Made in the USA
Middletown, DE
07 July 2025